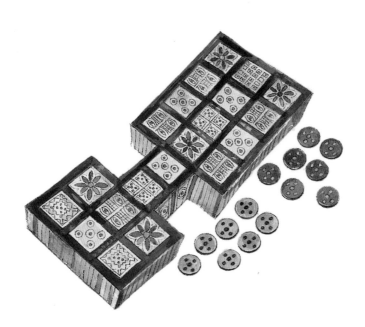

Author:
Jacqueline Morley studied English at
Oxford University. She has taught English and
history and now works as a freelance writer.
She has written historical fiction and nonfiction
for children.

Artist:
David Antram was born in Brighton, England,
in 1958. He studied at Eastbourne College of Art
and then worked in advertising for fifteen years
before becoming a full-time artist. He has
illustrated many children's nonfiction books.

Series Creator:
David Salariya was born in Dundee,
Scotland. He has illustrated a wide range of books
and has created and designed many new series for
publishers both in the UK and overseas. In 1989,
he established The Salariya Book Company. He
lives in Brighton with his wife, illustrator Shirley
Willis, and their son Jonathan.

Editor:
Sophie Izod

Editorial Assistant:
Mark Williams

© The Salariya Book Company Ltd MMVII

Published in Great Britain in 2007 by
The Salariya Book Company Ltd
25 Marlborough Place, Brighton BN1 1UB

ISBN-13: 978-0-531-18728-9 (Lib. Bdg.) 978-0-531-18921-4 (Pbk.)
ISBN-10: 0-531-18728-4 (Lib. Bdg.)   0-531-18921-X (Pbk.)

Published in 2007 in the United States
by Franklin Watts
An imprint of Scholastic Library Publishing
90 Sherman Turnpike, Danbury, CT 06816

A CIP catalog record for this book is available
from the Library of Congress.

Printed and bound in China.
Printed on paper from sustainable sources.

You Wouldn't Want to Be a Sumerian Slave!

Written by
Jacqueline Morley

Illustrated by
David Antram

Created and designed by
David Salariya

A Life of Hard Labor You'd Rather Avoid

Franklin Watts
A Division of Scholastic Inc.
NEW YORK • TORONTO • LONDON • AUCKLAND • SYDNEY
MEXICO CITY • NEW DELHI • HONG KONG
DANBURY, CONNECTICUT

Contents

Introduction

You're growing up on a farm in Sumeria in a part of the world that's known today as Iraq. Long ago it was called Mesopotamia, which means "the land between the rivers." Your people, the Sumerians, live in the southern part of Mesopotamia, some in cities and some in the countryside outside the city walls. You are not united under one ruler, like the ancient Egyptians; each city has its own king, who is often also its high priest. He rules as much land around his city as he can defend, which often means making war against neighboring cities. When this happens, life as a Sumerian peasant can be dangerous. It's a tough life anyway, but watch out, it could get tougher! If things go really wrong, you could end up as a Sumerian slave!

Map showing location of Sumer in relation to modern-day countries

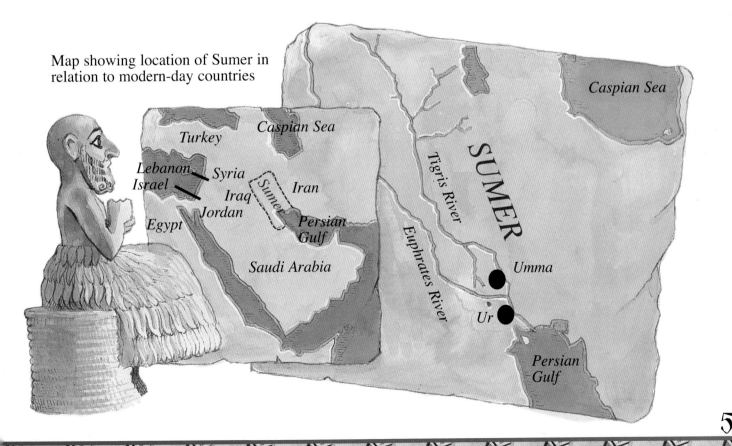

Caspian Sea

Turkey

Caspian Sea

Lebanon
Israel

Syria

Iran

Iraq

Sumer

Jordan

Egypt

Persian
Gulf

Saudi Arabia

Tigris River

SUMER

Euphrates River

Umma

Ur

Persian
Gulf

A Family Farmstead

Your farmstead's quite large because your father's brothers, their wives and children live with you too. Each family has its own living quarters grouped around the family yard. Everything is built of homemade mud bricks, plastered over, so when it crumbles it's easy to rebuild. The doors and windows open out onto the yard. A plain back wall links the houses together to form a safe enclosure. The whole family shares the farm work. As soon as you could walk, you were taking care of the geese or scaring birds away from the crops. Now you're the family's goatherd, and there's nothing you don't know about goats.

INSIDE there's a mat on the earth floor and a platform by the wall to sleep on. Apart from a few cooking pots, storage jars, and the stool your father sits on as head of the family, there's little else.

THE FLOOR often needs new layers of earth to keep it level with the yard which gets built up with dirt and trash. A higher floor will keep water from seeping inside. The roof, made of clay over matting, needs recoating every year too.

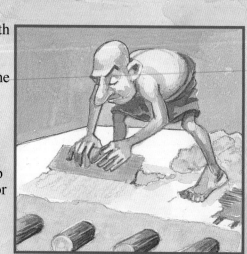

A frieze from a temple c.2500 BC

Handy Hint

Don't bother reclaiming old bricks. If your house has collapsed, level it, and build on top. Then it will be well clear of the yard (at first, anyway).

Flood and Drought

Things aren't easy for Sumerian farmers. The rivers flood at exactly the worst time of year: just as the crops are emerging. If the water's not controlled, the new shoots get washed away. Later in the year there is a long drought, just when the fields need water most. There has to be a well-organized system of canals and ditches to hold the water and move it to the fields when needed. Each family is responsible for keeping the ditches on their land in good repair.

OXEN are used for plowing and to drag a harrow over lumpy ground to break it up. Your little sister sits on the harrow to add extra weight.

REEDY GROUND is too rough to plow. Oxen are put in leather boots to stomp down weeds, as well as the sharp stubble left after reeds are cut.

WHEN YOUNG BARLEY is growing well, sheep are put to graze on it. This makes it shorter stemmed and thicker, and the manure helps it grow.

Sumerian plows are designed to cut a furrow and sow seed at the same time. You pour seed into the funnel while your elder brother guides the plow. According to your father, you're pouring in too much!

Handy Hint

When your seed starts to sprout, say a prayer to Ninkilim, goddess of field mice, to beg her not to let them eat your crop.

Not so much! I'm not made of money you know!

IN THE DRY SEASON, farmers make breaks in the raised ditches that run around their fields, to pour water out onto the thirsty crops.

WATCH OUT. Don't overwater your barley. If you do it will turn a reddish color—a sure sign of a fatal fungal disease.

9

Sold to Pay a Debt

Things have gone badly on the farm this year. The harvest was poor, and taxes have been raised. On top of this, a neighbor has won a lawsuit against your family so you now owe them compensation. With no other way to pay this debt, your family decides to sell you. Fathers have complete control over their children, so there's no point in arguing. You're taken to the main market outside the city gate, where your father haggles with the slave dealer, who doesn't offer much for you.

THE KING has come up with lots of new taxes to pay for the current war being fought. Fishermen must now pay a tax on their catches, and farmers must pay a tax when their sheep are sheared—the wool is plucked out, not cut off.

MORE TAXES are due for divorce and death. Officials even come to the burial to claim unpaid tax! Tax is paid in goods such as barley, bread, or date wine (money has not yet been invented). If you can't pay, they seize your property and throw you in prison.

THE LAWSUIT was over one of your irrigation ditches which bordered a neighbor's field. You hadn't fixed its banks properly. He was furious when it sprang a leak and flooded his young corn.

A Household Slave

You've been bought as a temporary house slave by a city merchant, for a period of three years. His house seems very grand to you. It has several rooms on two floors and a paved yard with potted plants in the middle. The merchant has two wives because the first was barren, and they are bitter rivals. If one sends you for water, the other is sure to call you upstairs. It's hard to do the right thing with two people yelling at once. You rush with the water jar and trip on a plant pot. The result—disaster! The merchant decides you've got to go.

THE FIRST WIFE sleeps on a sheepskin and the second has a mat, but you sleep on a brick bench in the kitchen.

terracotta food mold

THE FAMILY ROOMS are upstairs. The first wife lounges about here shouting orders all day. She knows her husband will never divorce her. She has property of her own and if he does, he'll lose it.

THE SECOND WIFE runs the kitchen. She says you're useless. You can't even unmold a pudding properly.

Only an idiot would buy a goatherd! He's only fit to be with goats - get rid of him!

12

Goatherd to the Gods

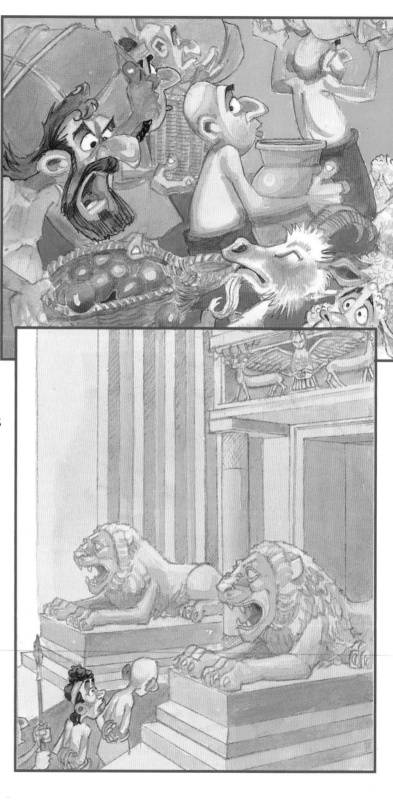

The temple overseer is at the market on the day the merchant returns you as faulty goods. He buys a number of slaves, including you. When you reach the temple, you realize why he needs a good goatherd—the courtyard is in chaos! Traders and customers struggle to get past the herds of sheep and goats brought as offerings to the goddess Inanna. Each city has its own guardian god or goddess, whose temple is its most important building. There are schools and workshops within its outer walls and it owns lots of land. Some of the animals you must manage are brought by tenant farmers as payment for the use of temple land.

YOU'VE NEVER been inside the temple gates before. Those lions don't look welcoming. You dread what the future holds for you.

AT LEAST you're doing a job you're really good at—getting unruly animals through tight spaces.

Handy Hint

Inspect the entrails when you sacrifice an animal. You can foretell the future from them.

THE IMAGE of the goddess stands in the temple's inner sanctuary. Votive statues surround it and priests offer it sacrificial meat.

THE LOST WAX PROCESS:

A

SUMERIANS are highly skilled at this. First they make a rough clay model.

B

NEXT they coat the clay with a layer of wax and carve in the fine details.

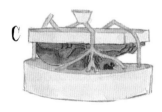

C

TUBES for pouring in liquid are attached, and everything is coated with clay.

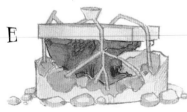

E

WHEN THE metal has cooled, the outer layer of clay is broken away.

F

THE TUBING is cut away and the casting is tooled and polished.

The Temple Workshops

You're in charge of a team of donkeys that carry materials to the temple workshops, then deliver the finished goods. All sorts of things needed by the temple—gold vessels, jewelry, furniture, leatherwork and cloth—are made here, in its workshops.

D

THE CLAY is then fired, melting the wax. Molten metal is then poured into the tubes.

IMPORTED materials (metal, stone, and wood) are weighed and recorded in each workshop.

STONEWORKERS can shape even the hardest rock using drills weighted with stones.

Transporting precious metal from the assay office to the workshops is a nerve-wracking job. It is weighed out to you in ingots, under the foreman's suspicious eyes. If the objects made from the metal weigh less than they did at the start, you may be accused of theft!

Handy Hint

Wood is scarce so reuse it. Three tabletops and four old boxes can be made into two beds and a brand-new box.

Enameled gold ring

GOLDSMITHS make delicate vessels, with chased decoration, out of beaten gold or silver.

FURNITURE makers produce elegant chairs and stools with animal-shaped legs.

FINEST VASES are made from metal, but potters also make storage jars and things for daily use.

TEXTILE WORKSHOPS employ large numbers of women, weaving tufted cloth and fine fabrics.

Keeping Records

The temple authorities keep records of all deliveries, so that they know exactly what the workshops have used. They also record all salaries and rations issued; and the exact number of animals, sacks of barley, and bales of wool brought to the temple as rent or tributes. These records are made by pressing marks into pieces of damp clay, which harden and are very long lasting. These are then kept in the temple's archive office.

> Hmm, I seem to be short of a hundred sheep!

THE BEGINNING OF WRITING: This clay tablet (right) from before 3000 BC shows objects that have been recorded by pictograms.

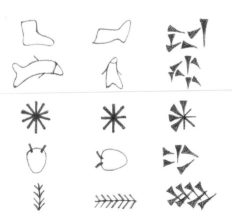

THE SUMERIANS developed what was probably the world's first writing system. They had the idea of using a pictogram to mean not only the object it resembled, but also other objects with similar sounding names. This developed into signs which represented syllables.

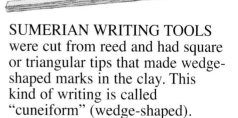

SUMERIAN WRITING TOOLS were cut from reed and had square or triangular tips that made wedge-shaped marks in the clay. This kind of writing is called "cuneiform" (wedge-shaped).

Try temple workshop's accounts.

Handy Hint

Get your father to treat your teacher to a meal. This has been known to make him give students much better reports.

Oh dear, that's not the same as mine.

FARMERS like you can't read or write, but if your family were rich, you would have gone to a temple school. Students spend a lot of time copying—there are hundreds of pictograms to learn.

DISCIPLINE IS STRICT. Boys who speak before they are spoken to, dress sloppily, stand up in class or leave the gate without permission, get beaten.

LATE FOR SCHOOL! The punctuality monitor is always at the door and will expect a good excuse if you're late.

War over Water

Your three years of slavery are nearly over, and you're looking forward to going home, when suddenly everything goes horribly wrong. Your city declares war on one of its neighbors, and you are drafted into the army. With your king leading the charge in his chariot, you all rush at the enemy. You are wearing only a leather cloak reinforced with metal disks for protection. But the enemy has a new tactic—a line of close-set shields you cannot break through. The battle is a disaster—you are taken prisoner, and that means slavery for life!

A Long-Standing Quarrel

FOR MANY YEARS there has been trouble between the two cities. Both kings claim an area between their cities that contains an important irrigation canal. Whoever controls it can cut off water from his rival's land. In a recent treaty, a third ruler forced them to agree to a boundary.

THE ENEMY KING decides to ignore the treaty. He knocks down the stele that marks the boundary.

HE THEN DIVERTS the canal so that lots of farmers, including your father, see their crops dry up and fail.

Handy Hint

To fully destroy a conquered city, carry off their guardian gods. Then they will be totally unprotected.

Oh dear, this doesn't look good.

AFTER THE BATTLE your king is made to kneel blindfolded before his foe, who puts his foot on his neck in triumph.

ENEMY SOLDIERS smash through the gates of your city, destroy its walls, and set fire to all the buildings.

WITH OTHER MISERABLE prisoners, you are put in a neck-stock and marched to slavery in your enemy's territory.

Hard Labor

Now you really learn what slavery's like! All day in the blazing sun you make mud bricks at a brick factory on a vast building site. Your captors have brought you to the great city of Ur, where the king, Ur-Nammu, has commanded the building of a magnificent new temple to his city's god. The temple itself will stand on a series of platforms, so that it seems to touch the sky. This type of the building is called a ziggurat. You can see it taking shape, brick by brick, in the distance.

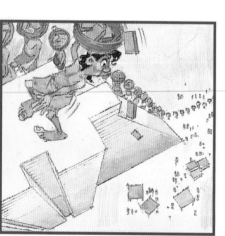

DELIVERING THE BRICKS is a nightmare. As the ziggurat grows higher, there are more and more steps to climb. The supporting platforms are a solid mass of brick.

YOU THINK you're lucky when you're transferred to canal digging. Raw hands and an aching back soon prove you wrong. You're digging out a 56-foot-wide channel.

Don't forget to add straw to the mixture of mud and water. If you don't, the bricks will crack as they dry.

Handy Hint

UR-NAMMU has ordered the building of four new canals. One will connect Ur with both the Euphrates River and the sea. This will mean that trading vessels can unload at the city's quays.

AT THE END of the day, you line up for your food ration. Workers get a fixed amount to eat, according to the jobs they do. It's usually fish, beer, and mush made from barley.

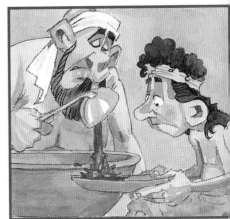

The Ziggurat Completed!

Even slaves get a day off when the whole city celebrates. Even though it's not your city and you'd give anything to get away from it, you can't help getting caught up in the excitement of the ziggurat's opening ceremony. Today the moon god, Nanna, guardian of Ur, is entering his new home. The king leads a procession of vassal kings, priests, and officials laden with offerings up the dizzying staircase.

BEFORE THE ziggurat was built, Ur-Nammu purified the site in a traditional ceremony in which he hammered in a ritual "foundation peg."

*copper peg
c.2100 BC*

LIMESTONE RELIEF c.2200 BC, showing a god inserting a foundation peg. Behind him a goddess prays for the well-being of the building.

Handy Hint
If you're invited to take part in the procession, seven sheep and seven goats is a suitable offering to bring.

UR-NAMMU MOUNTS the final stairway to the temple threshold. From here the high priestess of Nanna will lead him into the presence of the god.

DETAIL FROM the stele of King Ur-Nammu (ruled from 2112-2095 BC), showing him making an offering of drink to the moon god, Nanna.

A Feast for Nanna

The ceremony at the temple is followed by a great banquet at the palace. Sumerians believe that gods have the same appetites as humans. Therefore, the best way to please them is to give a feast in their honor, and to enjoy it on their behalf! Ur-Nammu and his queen host a lavish meal with lots of wine and barley-beer. Guests drink the beer straight from the jar, using tubes that filter out the stuff that settles at the bottom. Ordinary people celebrate too, as best they can, but not you. You have been given extra kitchen duties, so you just get to sneak a view from a passageway.

CELEBRATE. There's lots of lively music and songs to keep the party going. Dancers perform to pipes and drums and a harpist sings fantastic songs about the gods.

GAMES. Guests who prefer a quieter time can pit their wits against each other at board games.

For a tasty dish fit for a feast, add plenty of garlic, onions, and leeks. Sumerians love them.

Board game found in Sumerian tomb

Slaves of the Gods

You should be back in the kitchen, but you want to hear the end of a harpist's song. He tells how the gods hated work so much, they created humans to be their slaves. But the humans they created made so much noise that Enlil, father of the gods, decided to destroy them. Only one god, Enki, was on the humans' side. He warned a very good man, named Atrahasis, that Enlil planned to send a terrible flood to wipe out mankind. Atrahasis built an ark and filled it with his family, his workmen, and every useful domestic and wild creature. These survived the flood and repopulated the Earth.

THE SUN was dark; the flood roared like a bull. Atrahasis' ark was tossed in the tempest for six days and seven nights.

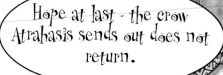

Hope at last - the crow Atrahasis sends out does not return.

Glossary

Archive office Place where written records are kept.

Ark Large ship.

Assay office Place where various metals are weighed and tested.

Barren Unable to have children.

Chase To add a decorative pattern to metal by using tools that raise or mark its surface.

Compensation A payment made, or action taken, to make amends for damage or loss to someone.

Frieze A band of decoration that runs along a wall.

Harrow A large log or heavy wooden frame, dragged over plowed land to break up clods of earth or cover seed.

Ingot A mass of metal that has been shaped into a block or bar.

Irrigation The process of bringing water to crops by means of artificial channels.

Lawsuit Bringing a civil case against someone in a court of law.

Monitor A person who oversees students' conduct in school.

Neck-stock A timber frame enclosing a prisoner's neck, to stop them from escaping.

Quay A place built specifically for the purpose of loading and unloading boats.

Ritual A set of actions that is always performed in the same way as part of a religious ceremony.

Sanctuary The innermost, most sacred part of a temple where the gods were thought to live.

Seal A small object of metal or another hard substance, engraved with an official design, that was used for stamping a mark on soft wax. This showed that a document had come from an official source.

Seal impression The mark made by a seal.

Stele An upright slab featuring a sculpted design or inscription.

Temporary Not lasting forever.

Terracotta Unglazed pottery made of brownish-red clay.

Tribute A gift or payment to a god or a ruler.

Vassal A person or ruler who must submit services or gifts to another more powerful ruler.

Vizier A high-ranking assistant or advisor.

Votive Something offered or dedicated to a god or goddess.

Index